Inspired by memories of time spent
with my parents and sister
along the shores of Lake Ontario.

• • •

WHEN THE WAVES SUBSIDE

THERE IS HOPE

Lisa M. Buske

http://LisaMBuske.com
Email: lbuskewriter@aol.com

Photography and Photographic Enhancements by Lisa M. Buske

Scripture taken from the Holy Bible, New International Version®, NIV®. Copyright © 1973, 1978, 1984, 2011 by Biblica, Inc.™ Used by permission of Zondervan. All rights reserved worldwide. **www.zondervan.com** The "NIV" and "New International Version" are trademarks registered in the United States Patent and Trademark Office by Biblica, Inc.™

ISBN 978-0615759449

• • •

Dedication Page
To my parents, Ken and Sue Allen.

In 1994, tragedy ripped your youngest daughter
and my only sister, Heidi M. Allen, from our lives.

Thank you for modeling strength, determination, and love
on a daily basis ~ especially the days since Heidi's kidnapping.

Thank you for raising both your girls.
We might not see Heidi again on this side of heaven,
yet our memories keep her alive in our hearts.

• • •

"I will lead the blind

by ways they have not known,

along unfamiliar paths.

I will guide them;

I will turn the darkness

into light before them

and make the rough places smooth.

These are the things I will do;

I will not forsake them."

Isaiah 42:16 NIV

• • •

• • •

Preface

    In 1994, my only sister, Heidi M. Allen, worked alone at the local convenience store on Easter Sunday. While most people enjoyed Easter celebrations with their family and friends, my family and community searched for my missing sister. Heidi was kidnapped on the third of April and remains missing to this day.

    The idea for this book came to me on a smoldering afternoon, while listening to John Stumbo preach at *Delta Lake Bible Conference* in Rome, New York. He asked us to share our analogy on life with him. I didn't come up with anything right away but with prayer, it became clear.

    God blessed me with an analogy to share with Mr. Stumbo before leaving camp and ignited the idea for this book. I don't claim to understand how my parents felt after the loss of their youngest daughter, yet I do see how they changed. This is how I saw tragedy change my parents since Heidi's disappearance over eighteen years ago.

    Photographs of some of our glass rocks are within this book as a reminder that once-broken shards have potential to become more beautiful because of the waves beating against them. Just like my parents!

• • •

· · ·

Your father and I met in July 1970 on a blind date at New Haven Field Days. The next day we took a walk on the beach by Bramas camp. I shared with your dad about collecting "glass stones" as a child. It started us that day looking for "glass stones". We have added to the jar over almost 40 yrs. We took alot of beach walks back then cause couldn't afford to much else but we wanted to be together. Over the years we picked them up on vacations or other times. When you and Heidi were little we'd take you to look for the precious "glass stones". It's a good memory for your dad and I seeing your happy faces when you found one. Also buggying down to beach with Mary so she has added some to the jar of Allen's glass stones.

This is the note written by my Mom in 2007 when she passed one collection of glass rock treasures to my daughter and me on Christmas morning. Actual photographs of our glass rocks are throughout the book. Priceless heirlooms...

• • •

Lake Ontario, Mexico Point Park, New York

The tradition started with just the two,
left to walk the beach, when the money was through.
They never complained, but held each other's hand,
because they knew their love could withstand.

After the wedding and birth of their girls,
it was time to introduce the kids to the swirls.
The same lake shore from date nights of past,
transitioned to family time, and memories to last.

Trips to the shore showed our parent's love and care.
The aroma of Lake Ontario permeated the air;
Its breeze served as a reminder of time spent together.
My sister and I learned the outdoors is something to treasure.

Most of these adventures were just with us four.
With my parents leading the way to the rocky shore.
Giggles on piggy-back down Dempster Beach Drive,
fueled our tight bond that helped our family thrive.

• • •

Once at the lake, the fun and search began,
we needed a smooth rock, to hold in our hand.
Shouts of glee and giggles of joy echoed for all to hear,
When beneath a larger stone, did the perfect rock appear.

Thousands of stones and rocks nestled on the beach,
dad pointed to a few, just the right size within our reach.
While Mom crouched to find a new rock for our collection,
these little treasures evidence of a mother's affection.

Priceless excursions blessed our family through the years,
stones were skipped and others brought home, for souvenirs.
Dad encompassed our hands and taught us how to throw,
mom's patience to sift through the pebbles, a gift to sow.

• • •

This tradition started as soon as we could walk,
moments of silence transitioned into times to talk.
Secrets were shared and dreams explored,
the love for each other couldn't be ignored.

Through the years of toddler to teen,
we recognized a new aspect of the scene.
Our ability to skip a stone and count its hops,
became a challenge to win, with our dear Ol' Pops.

A competitive edge kept us strong and determined,
our parents love was more than we imagined.
When the skipping finished and we fell to our knees,
mom moved the stones aside with no guarantees.

With each gentle stroke to remove the stones,
mom shared wisdom, and life's potential unknowns.
We never thought kidnapping a possibility,
instead dreams and plans with invincibility.

Mom and Dad listened with joyful delight,
to know their daughters knew not to fight.
Each moment together is a precious gift,
one to take advantage of, before a life shift.

This is what happened to our family in '94,
my sister went to work and was found no more.
Mom and Dad lost more than their child,
security, trust, and fear were riled.

I watched their hair turn grey before my eyes,
regressing frames and illness, they couldn't disguise.
They never give up and keep living for the day,
for they know it's what their precious Heidi would say.

· · ·

They live the lessons taught so many years before,
while skipping stones and finding rocks, along the lake's shore.
The glass rocks hidden beneath the stones,
have been beaten and tossed into dark unknowns.

My parents will never be the same because of their pain,
yet their beauty and strength never do wane.
Like the broken bottles turned into treasured rocks of glass,
both are evidence they survived the brokenness of their past.

• • •

When the Waves Subside

There is Hope

Other Books by Lisa M Buske
Where's Heidi? One Sister's Journey

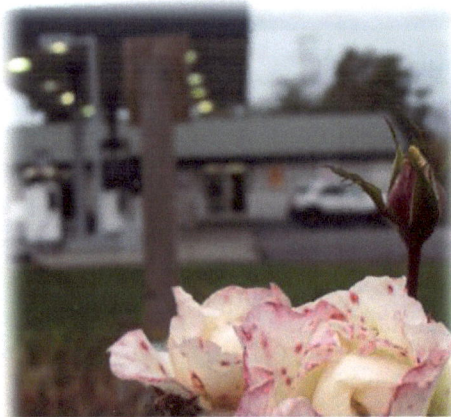

Where's Heidi?

Lisa M. Buske

April 3, 2013 Release Date

http://LisaMBuske.com
http://www.lisambuske.com/blog.html

Email: lbuskewriter@aol.com
Facebook, Pinterest, & LinkedIn:
Lisa M. Buske
Twitter: @LisaBuske
Facebook: "Where's Heidi?"

Mailing: P.O. Box 261, New Haven, New York 13121

• • •

www.ingramcontent.com/pod-product-compliance
Lightning Source LLC
Chambersburg PA
CBHW042100040426
42448CB00002B/79

* 9 7 8 0 6 1 5 7 5 9 4 4 9 *